The WOMAN SHOE

UNSHATTERED GLASS

W*The*MAN SHOE

UNSHATTERED GLASS

Una Kumba Thompson

Senior Publisher
Steven Lawrence Hill Sr

ASA Publishing Corporation

ASA Publishing Corporation
An Accredited Hybrid Publishing House with the BBB
www.asapublishingcorporation.com

The Landmark Building
23 E. Front St., Suite 103, Monroe, Michigan 48161

All Rights Reserved. No part of this publication may be reproduced, stored in a retrieval system or transmitted in any form or by any means electronic, mechanical, photocopying, recording or otherwise, without the prior written permission of the publisher. Author/writer rights to "Freedom of Speech" protected by and with the "1st Amendment" of the Constitution of the United States of America. This is a work of non-fiction; educational learning in women rights. Any resemblance to actual events, locales, person living or deceased that is not related to the author's literacy is entirely coincidental.

With this title/copyrights page, the reader is notified that the publisher does not assume, and expressly disclaims any obligation to obtain and/or include any other information other than that provided by the author, unless permitted. Any belief system, promotional motivations, including but not limited to the use of non-fictional/fictional characters and/or characteristics of this book, are within the boundaries of the author's own creativity in order to reflect the nature and concept of the book.

Any and all vending sales and distribution not permitted without full book cover and this copyrights page.

Copyrights©2018 Una Kumba Thompson, All Rights Reserved
Book Title: The Woman Shoe *Unshattered Glass*
Date Published: 01.29.2018 / Edition 1 *Trade Paperback*
Book ID: ASAPCID2380732
ISBN: 978-1-946746-10-8
Library of Congress Cataloging-in-Publication Data

This book was published in the United States of America
Great State of Michigan

Publisher's Trademark Copyrights Page

DEDICATION

This book is dedicated to my mother Mrs. Mildred Soko Watta Gbegbe who looked forward to celebrating the publishing of my book with great anticipation, but did not live to see it happen. Her life's journey serves as an inspiration for what women can overcome, empowered by who they are by nature and who they become by nurture, to grow into their very own best. I am because of her and I am grateful for such a wonderful mother.

ACKNOWLEDGMENT

I want to thank my children who helped me with their encouragement, conversation and commitment: Mrs. *Rokia Ouattara Okai, Ms. Larissa Oubly Lekpai,* Mrs. *Samuna Soko Massa Thompson-Wreh,* Dr. Mrs. *Rochelle Taade Thompson-Kolawole,* Mr. *Samuel Wonwi Thompson,* and *Ms. Una Angelique Thompson.*

I would also like to thank the following people: *Steven Lawrence Hill Sr* for his guidance and insights and *Gerry Roberts,* who provided an opportunity for me to attend a book boot camp which helped me take the first step in becoming an Author.

My appreciation to family and friends, especially Mr. *Dempster Yallah,* Mr. *Duma Jensen,* Mr. *Rufus Thompson,* Mrs. *Yamah Momolu Zaza,* Mrs. *Josephine Lackey Northam* and Mrs. *Florence Thomson Sirleaf* for cheering me on and being my support team.

To God is the Glory from whom all my blessings come!!!

Table of Contents

Dedication ....
Acknowledgment .... a
Table of Contents i
Introduction 3

Chapter 1 By Design or Creation 5
- **What do you see when you see a woman?**

Chapter 2 Separating Truth from What We Perceive 19
- **We are all architects**

Chapter 3 Whose Shoe is it Anyway 41
- **Rights and Choice**

Chapter 4 Let Me Breathe 61
- **Kill Suppression, Oppression, Sexism**

Chapter 5 In Equality We Rise 75
- **Women's Rights is Centerline**

Chapter 6 At the Feet of Every Woman 83
- **Find Yourself**

Chapter 7 A World Visa **91**
- Violence, Sex, Abuse

Chapter 8 Breaking the Code of Silence **101**
- It's His Shame Not Yours

Chapter 9 Politics, Power & Women **111**
- The Male Factor

Chapter 10 Women Unite **125**
- Unity of Purpose

Research References **133**

The WOMAN SHOE
UNSHATTERED GLASS

Una Kumba Thompson

INTRODUCTION

This book is to encourage a somber reflection with the aim of Inspiring, Educating, and Empowering to help break away from and dismantle societal constructs that hinder and limit the natural growth, potentials, and progress of women. It is to inspire us to look beyond negative stereotypes and change our perceptions and behaviors within the world order in regard to women, and break the cycle of patriarchy.

Seeing a woman rightly and having a better society, that treats women with equity, are intertwined and inseparable to development.

Discovering false illusions, that masculinity means that a man is superior and all-powerful, as femininity is a woman being inferior and weak, overshadows the rights and abilities of women, and widens the doorway to longstanding gender inequalities.

This narrative is geared towards shedding light on a society made up of people with developed systems who live together as human beings but are failing to ensure equality for both women and men by the oneness of humankind.

It is to bring a deeper understanding to the pain and agony that women suffer at the hands of injustice, the abuse of their rights, including violence and sexual assaults.

To walk in a woman's shoe may not be glamorous or easy but the willpower to step into it shows the glamour and humanity of societies that can be an engine to change the status quo for a better world for all.

This book is also intended to challenge you to a journey and question what you imagined a woman to be.

CHAPTER 1

By Design or Creation

What do you see when you see a woman?

When you are at home, at work, in school, and when you go to a grocery store, carrying on daily chores, when you travel, interact with people, in and around your surroundings, and see or look at a female, what is the first thought that comes to your mind? How do you see her; who do you actually see? What kind of internal reaction do you get when your thoughts interact with the question?

Let's be assured that there is no right or wrong answer to this question. It is for you to know within yourself what thought came to mind at that moment. Whether you got an answer, or everything just went blank for a second, no worries.

So, prepare yourself for a mind changing and freedom ride as we uncover the "hidden" woman, and how you should envision her. Brace yourselves!

The task is to help us reflect on our thoughts as we go about everyday life accepting that men and women are not born to be equal within the placement of society. It is to take a personal journey to search within ourselves for beliefs and perceptions about women and envision our perspective, individually and collectively.

To understand these thought processes, you have to be open minded in first taking a closer look at the way women and men are socialized by different standards within the family unit, the community and greater society.

You may agree, disagree, or even reject it, but when for a moment you think about your own family and the roles assigned to the female in that home setting as compared to the male, you will realize that indeed the female is not measured on par with the male in the household.

Because she is perceived as a lesser gender, it is accept negative or different treatment of her, and the unjustifi reasons which have the propensity to perpetuate and solidify biases against her.

The way society portrays women is a major factor in the wrongful way men often perceive women without any remorse, regardless of the socio-economic and political evolution of strength women have shown, long before the women's rights movement began. The lingering question is whether society is willing to accept the evolution of women to be independent and equal, or has it refused to make rational assessment on how truly women are viewed and why men rarely think about the inequality of a woman, moreover finding it difficult to accept that she is really an equal?

It is therefore no surprise that the governing bodies and structures for the advancement of society and world at large are established based on patriarchal values that are deeply entrenched into homes and the fabric of our culture, religion, education, and tradition. This causes discrimination and the demeaning of women without thought. Consequently, we have a society geared towards building environments that not only cultivate repressive and superior attitudes in men but reinforce beliefs that they are the masters over women. With this kind of orientation, men will likely be immune to the suffering of women, lacking the empathy that guards against negative perceptions in their mindset.

This is not what was meant to be. The world was not created for the male alone, neither was he to be the ruler and king with the woman as his subordinate, captive to serve at his will and pleasure.

The biblical saying goes that "because of lack of knowledge, my people perish." There is so much truth to this. The most frightening fact remains that when information meant to enlighten is put before our very eyes, we opt to trash it as unimportant because it does not fit within our stereotypes. False teachings and misinformation about who a woman is supposed to be are applauded and reinforced, while facts and information on the best of her are distorted and buried to sustain the status quo. This is a pathway to living with an untruthful answer and wrong reasoning towards them.

The existence and life of one so precious has not been placed into society as an equal, if not intentionally, then only as the causality of the visual manifestation that it's simply a woman. The fact is, she is not simply a woman and is obviously more than the female perceived by the opposite sex.

A flawed society designed by men has an inharmonic balance of socialization, discouraging the development of women, her exercise of rights, and her enjoyment of liberty. We have a society that thrives on the exclusion of women from any form or source of power, authority, and stature. It is deemed unrealistic, if not forbidden, for her to rise and have freedom since that diminishes the boundaries of male dominance. The portrayal that women have no place in an authoritative position, that their fate is doomed, is silently embraced and subtly introduced within formal and informal learning institutions.

By so doing, we are validating this erroneous line of thought: that within the natural order, within the infinite wisdom and intentions of God, a man was created to be superior to a woman, she was created as an unequal human being. These mistaken thoughts, misconceptions, interpretations, and teachings of society have conditioned men to mentally obey the dictates of that society to the detriment of women.

Why did society stoop so low and how did it reach this point one may wonder? Simply told, it is because the values, beliefs, and principles enshrined in the learning processes are designed to undermine the humanity *of society* and impede the advancement and empowerment of women for an equal, peaceful, and *cooperative community*. From an early age we are introduced into either religious, cultural, or traditional beliefs that in many instances are an anti- woman toxin and are harmful to their well-being.

As an example, "You do not have to be religious to know what is being subconsciously taught across the dinner table or by watching as the woman approaches from the kitchen in servanthood, in this simple fashion." This is one of many visual stimuli to teach what type of manifestation of positions a woman has been stereotyped into, thus causing this role to seem like the natural arrangement of things in society and a reason to become insensitive and blind to the strength, power, and dignity of a woman. This perpetuates how a woman is stereotyped and perceived on a daily basis.

There are key elements in every societal structure that determine how we are socialized and that influence our way of life, like tradition, culture, religion, beliefs, and values. These are pillars upon which our socialization depends for the development of people and advancement of society in general. But the way the systems are setup and the manner in which they work and operate, have proven to be not in the best interest of women. They are unfavorable and often groom men to have a negative mindset that perceive women as the lesser, compared to a man; just a "mere woman", not more than just that. This gives false reasons to validate the belief that women should not be counted as equals and ignore the effect this has.

The structures and systems that are setup within society are meant for the purpose of developing and molding people's minds, bodies, and souls to say the least in an organized and systemic approach. Society is entrusted with the responsibility to ensure that men and women are socialized to conform and fit into society; abiding to the authority of government and getting involved in activities.

In this process, we see that men are in charge and predominantly responsible for how we are socialized at all levels which makes it seemed natural to treat people differently with a set of standards that spells INEQUALITY from day one.

When the system favors men, puts men in charge, and the

tenets of socialization are discriminatory against women, your perception of who a woman is will definitely be as you are taught; most likely, not a high opinion.

Sometimes in our comfort zones we find solace in feeling and believing that all human beings are created equal, which is correct. The reality is that society prohibits real equality for women. Don't wave it off. Think on what came to your mind when the question was asked "What do you see when you see a woman?" Then decide if you agree or disagree about the reality presented that society prohibits real equality for women.

Why we rarely consider questioning ourselves about our thoughts and perceptions of equality between men and women are due to denial of its relevance to our daily lives and being raised to know that men are stronger and more important than women.

Are there a different set of standards for women? Did we surpass human rights and allow undignified women human rights to perpetuate societal causes of a certain order, or a political and abusive pattern that accumulate and perpetuate a male supremacy?

Do we see the imbalances, inequities, and inequalities in the structures and systems that allow men to have social status, political power, and resources over women in the way we think? Are women rising to power only to be still looked down upon? Do others accept bare positions that produce unjustifiable and unequal pay that favors men, i.e. same position but the male gets a higher pay grade?

The mother is looped into a system and given the burden to provide primary care, being regarded as weak, while the father, who gives minimum care or has neglected that side of his responsibilities, voluntarily or involuntarily is considered strong.

This is a scenario that shows the distortion of the natural order in society where the man is seen as strong, more productive and acting rightly in his natural element while the woman is stereotyped and punished for behaving in a similar natural order of things. It is an unfair balance that is ignored by society and devalues the ability of women even on a small scale. The blame is not solely in the culture, tradition, or religion as assumed, but on patriarchal ideology and traditions that are conditioned to put the woman in the kitchen, not carrying a briefcase, or having the courage to perform tasks equal to or more than a man. But surely, from a rightfully natural and social standpoint, the woman has the resilience, ability, tenacity, and is endowed with inner strength beyond comprehension.

The people make up society, but what has society subconsciously or consciously diagramed and taught about the two kinds of humans, the male and female created in "Gods image" to have dominion over the earth?

By Design or Creation!!!

What do you see when you see a woman?

CHAPTER 2

Separating Truth from What We Perceive
We are all architects

The religious orientation that the woman is the weaker person and the man the stronger has been translated to mean *Power,* and with power comes control over women, access to wealth and resources including opportunities for leadership, decision making and other social status. It is no wonder that society has not made meaningful strides in changing the mindset of men and remove obstacles to women's empowerment.

Think of being in one of the well-respected high-level positions that you can imagine. Then consider how you are perceived. Take that perception and equate its strength to your supporters including people from other countries who look up to you in that position. Imagine you're running for office. Better yet, imagine you're a woman in a presidential race in America and you are so close to becoming the next President of the United States. Think about it for a moment. That's an extraordinary feat to accomplish and you're almost there tapping on its door. Then you hear something so bizarre that your hopes of being the next President of the United States starts to feel inevitable.

Here is a Washington Post Editorial written by David A. Fahrenthold on October 8th, 2016. When you read this, please take into consideration that this is a man with authority, social status and economic power.

"I moved on her, and I failed. I'll admit it," Trump is heard saying. It was unclear when the events he was describing took place. The tape was recorded several months after he married his third wife, Melania.

"Whoa," another voice said.

"I did try and f--- her. She was married," Trump says.

Trump continues: "And I moved on her very heavily. In fact, I took her out furniture shopping. She wanted to get some furniture. I said, 'I'll show you where they have some nice furniture.'"

"I moved on her like a bitch, but I couldn't get there. And she was married," Trump says. "Then all of a sudden, I see her, she's now got the big phony tits and everything. She's totally changed her look."

A woman in the presidential race; wow, your chance of becoming president increased and became great right? But unfortunately, a chauvinistic society does not have stalls for the politically correct, only for the source of power that is directed in a "manly" position because when the election was over, we saw who was left standing and the one who was forced into conceding and yielding to defeat. There's nothing more hurtful than witnessing the climax of male chauvinism and prejudice against a person because she is a woman, a viewpoint that solidifies testimonial after testimonial to a society that is biased against women. It rewards men with more power, especially those with authority and affluence, for inflicting pain, exploitation, and violence against women and encourages both men and women to reject gender equality and accountability. Whether a woman is slave or free, any origin of color, it doesn't matter, the deck was stacked since nearly the beginning of time without reason, only with false justification of superiority.

We need to backtrack our steps to the obsolete man because we now know that something has lost its way. Man moved from being a gentleman to a woman, to disrespecting her. And this goes for any age of male species. Women are simply the lesser, of no great importance. Our subconscious has taken away the human rights of a woman simply by society brushing off its humanity.

This epidemic seemed to grow in a manner of catastrophic proportions. Even Europeans, African, Asian and many men around the world at all levels of social strata, see women in condescending ways and as objects for male gratification, whether by verbal expression or the grabbing of the arm as a natural acceptable behavior.

The claims to love, honor, and cherish may not have its value walking across the aisle due to how we were subconsciously taught without even thinking hard. A man knew that he was in control, all power belongs to him. Children know that the father is supposed to be the bread winner. Anything out the ordinary would portray a male as weak and not man enough in the community and society.

Do you see how governance comes into play? Just to clarify for substance, the meaning for governance is having power or dominance over. Because men have managed to manipulate the laws of a sovereign and just God, they have clothed themselves as judges, jurors and executioners with power invested in them to dominate women and the world. As a result, society is what it is and exactly what it allowed patriarchy itself to do: to impose supremacy over women without even thinking twice. And why? Because we are doing it so well subconsciously as a natural order, an everyday way of life, men and women.

When a woman is thinking that she cannot move further in life, it's usually at times associated with domestic abuse, misogyny or some form of traditional barrier embedded her position. She doesn't see pass the milestone, only what is before her and how she can be pleasing without causing or ruffling a few feathers. This is an indirect example of a woman overwhelmed with the pressure of living a life constrained as an inferior. She sees no hope; the odds are too much to bear.

Now don't be misled to believe that she is weak, or has rights that are an extension of human rights and therefore she is protected. As is it a falsified security and reinforces a position that a man is the protector and not the law. Since the dawning of time when God said "Let there be light" so-to-speak, God did not intend for a woman to fight for rights as creatures of humankind equal in

His sight. It is rather an abused law of God which was absorbed into the law of the land where men made it into an unnatural law. Now, as we see today, it is automatically formulated on the tablets of our hearts, from childhood to adulthood, without much questioning that its right to impose an inferiority status on women.

In 1848, the Women's Rights Movement began and seemed to help motivate women's lives and change the way of thinking. They realized that their voices mattered and were soon to be heard. But the background note on this political position still had an unsavory twist to it. Long after its victory, men were still the decision makers. In general, there was still that final decision left to a man, carefully designed against women being an equal.

Makes you wonder just how women's rights still feel like it's not connected to human rights. After all, they should go hand in hand. In any case, it's just not so. A fabricated extension arm from human rights still has a foot on the elbow, causing disappointment to women despite some successes.

There is something like a thick glass ceiling hanging overhead that still gives women a feeling of vulnerability and helplessness as the day a woman walked out of the kitchen and into the employment environment. The glass is in need of shattering to destroy the false illusion that a woman that walks on earth is broken and must be held in mental and physical captivity because she is inferior, fragile, and weak.

To classify a person as inferior mean you want them broken. Now this *broken* implies one that accepts defeat and takes on the mold of tolerance and obedience from an authoritative figure and the surrounding social atmosphere. The message is "break the woman; she is inferior", which is a far cry away from human rights as she is not treated as a human being.

Does a woman have a right to speak, voice an opinion or for anything at all? Most may say that she does but get this, if she speaks in a tone that shows signs of authority, confidence, or courage then she may have crossed the limitations; limits that touch the cross-point of manhood. Imagine a woman desiring a position for political office but with different strings attached to ensure she never sees the fruition of it. This shows abuse of power discrimination and marginalization. Where does enjoyment of rights fit into the grand plan of human rights, let alone to say women's rights?

That's the real basic question. Where? Well, technically it does without conflict as long as a woman would know her boundaries. Cruel, yes, but this is how being nurtured and groomed in a "man's world" has eroded a woman's right, from time to time, until it became much easier to accept as natural way of life.

The Women Movement Activists and Feminists are battling to change the architecture of society, until a male pre-dominant rule, which is bent on ensuring patriarchy, is uprooted. We need to eradicate a mindset of men who want never to forget their rightful inheritance as head and not the tail, as having all rights to liberty, freedom, and choice for a fulfilled life. These and many more belong to him and at his will and pleasure can give or bestow to a woman.

Women know this is a lie from the East to West, North to South, even as society tries to sustain this fallacy. Women know that this is not true, and men know it as well. It may have taken a long time for women to realize and fully comprehend that the one who rules your body, mind, and soul is your master.

Women know that they, along with men, own this world equally and have a right to building an inclusive, safe, and wholesome functioning society where everyone can dwell.

They are determined to break the glass ceiling of male bigotry, misogyny, and domination.

This is playing a role in the movement for women's rights. Though at times some women do not know where they belong other than where society has placed them, while others want to dismantle the ugly structures of patriarchy in every sphere of society.

- *If you're a woman, what molds you to become a person of freedom?*
- *If you're a man, what molds you to become a person*

of freedom?

We can see color, religion, ethnic, and many other listings in freedom, and we cannot see women in freedom, at least not the way it was meant to be: equal!

One would have thought that women have gained the power of freedom within the laws of human rights and other legal instruments for the rights of women and gender equality and that women hold validity within the purpose and texture of governance. But understand what happened to one of the most powerful and influential woman in the world, who was about to become a president of the United States of America. A country where ugly has reared its head and the political rise of a woman has openly shown just how difficult it is to shatter the glass of patriarchy and misogyny. Could we be bucking in a circumstance that is clearly becoming out of control?

In any case there is surely a struggle for something. It's definitely not a struggle just to regain lost hope in a society discriminating against women but to unite women for their common good. The struggle is for power, authority and control. Men want to hold tight to what they perceive as birth rights and so the powers that be make women believe that they support removing impediments to achieving gender equality and women's rights. It's more about a political correctness, because much has happened only in theory but in practice.

Men know that full equality for women will include equal sharing of power, authority and wealth and this was never in the grand scheme of plans. How can this be possible? Men are panicking; they say it is inconceivable to sit a broken vessel on the highest supreme seat of society as an equal in all things! Then they plot because theirs is not to lead with justice, fairness and freedom but to rule, conquer and control for their ego and false superiority complex.

What this tells us is that the women struggle to change this paradigm in society is like chasing the wind. So long as society maintains its trends in favor of the man and until gender equality and women's rights become a fight not just by women but a joint fight with men of good conscience who believe in the inherent rights of every human being, we have got a way to go.

Yet we cannot continue to harbor tolerance for wrong and hold on to the thinking that women have to succumb to this fashion of inhumanity and classification. We must separate truth from what is false by allowing ourselves to assess a gathering of different situations and circumstances involving women that have caused and helped build a difficult walk path for them.

An example of such is a division of interpretation of choice and tradition where some women frown on those who choose to step out of the binds of traditional assigned roles. Women who opt to remain in ascribed positions challenge others who want to change.

Women, like men, are not a homogeneous species and cannot be expected to be the same. But because women have suffered a terrible blow to their individuality, claiming and exercising rights is a slippery path that also works against them as they strive to be in one accord and one voice.

Women see the fight not as a lost cause but like a noose placed around the neck of a woman who is trying to breathe air and not die. The fight is to live and choose a direction where women and men can equally find their rightful places and comfortably progress into society. The fight to breathe the breath of life without different standards set for women and without barriers that tend to negatively impact and affect their well-being.

It has been said that it's not always men that create the situation or circumstances that marginalize women or promote inequalities. This is the kind of propaganda intended to create a trail for us to scoop up and downplay the fact that we have a society that is male dominated. You can see how it is happening, how women become alienated and how it has evolved so uniquely unparalleled to any type of domination.

Women's rights are to fight for the idea that women should have equal rights with men. Over history, this has taken the form of gaining women's suffrage, to voting, holding property, reproductive control, and the right to work. When we look at the socio-economic trends of how these rights compare to their application, we see that society is unjust and that the trees have barricaded the rights of women but are allowing women to fight for the "idea" of it.

Then it is no more than injustice and prejudice within the inside of global society led by judicial and political correctness of countries in allowing the idea of women's rights and equality to just be heard. Women's rights, like all other rights, is not a culture, nor a traditional innuendo or suggestion, but a human rights and natural quest by all human kind among which are all manner of women.

The pioneers and the new generation of the feminist movement have had differences of opinions and philosophy since its birth in the struggle for rights and equality, but as a whole have remained united in this cause. This is because women are gradually awakening to the rude reality that fighting among themselves and failing to build chains of solidarity around their common agenda, can only sustain a patriarchal system. This can exclude and marginalize them even more, defeating the purpose for which we fight. In a society of male dominance, entrenched in patriarchal structures and systems, and established to be controlled by a man will not fully be revolutionized in disunity.

The people make up society, but what has society subconsciously taught the people about the two kinds of human species, the male and female created in "Gods image" destined to have "dominion over the earth"? *"Mary what's for dinner? . . . And where are my shoes?"* If the woman at home stops playing fetch, then the control will elevate its motive with a true meaning of what goes on outside of the box of love, and a welcome mat will be at the door to our not-really-so-newfound mannerism.

If a woman decides to make a choice in her pregnancy, there won't be a cast of votes, but an analytical lurking in that choice; a choice that will reach the political rooftops for a decision to handle the woman and her body.

This brings about the everyday truth that men, having dominated the planning of our society, were not interested in the best interest of the other half of the population.

The legal terminologies of rights say one thing, while their interpretation and implementation is a different ball game. Words of *Encouragement* and *Praises* for women standing up for themselves have come from all circles of male power. With a grain of satisfaction, their ego tells them that they have done well for the women, demonstrating how women and their issues are treated frivolously by society oblivious to the wrong and shame.

We are born into the optimism of life, the dictation of culture, religion, and an amplified patriarchal system that tells us the man is the working man, bread winner and king while the woman is the care giver, stand by your man and be who she is destined to be - inferior. To be otherwise is to become unnatural, therefore is deserved to be told and reminded that *"no matter what she is, she is still beneath the shoe of man".*

Before writing this book, I had not heard this lyric which speaks volumes to the realities of women. This has driven many women with potential and dreams to be subjected in the fashion as the less fortunate. If those lyrics resonate well with you, then you are deeply reflecting on what women around the world are faced with.

Women must continue to find the courage to fight the shackles of misogyny and dispel the lie that a woman is beneath the shoe of a man. She must have the hope of rising from the 'poor me' to clothe themselves with their own distinct colors of royalty, wisdom, nobility, equality, wealth, and freedom.

In this space and in this time, it can be said right now that suppression is not the keeper at the gate of society; it is the lack of acknowledgement that a woman is more. She is as an equal and integral part of the human race. The truth: Suppression is the blind side of the subconscious which holds and captivates the mindset of its caretaker.

Certainly, a new perception must emerge in order for society to retract its prejudicial elements against women. Nonetheless, we need to understand that the Creator of the universe did not intend to separate rights for human beings but to give them a choice within those rights to become the best of human kind.

Separating Truth from what we perceive!!!

We are all architects

CHAPTER 3

Whose Shoe is it Anyway
Rights and Choice

A darker side of society had long since turned a deaf ear to the ideals of the women's movement which is the engine and catalyst for the rights of women and gender equality. What made it difficult is the fact that advocacy for human rights was becoming unglued to the basic principles and the very fabric of what it is all about: shortchanging the fundamentals of women's rights.

This causation has brewed bitter concerns in the women's movement because those flaws had seemed not too optimistic or favorable to women.

This brings to mind that women alone cannot dismantle patriarchy for a balanced, just, and equal society. It is ironic, and it should speak to the very core of our hearts.

Over a period of time society has injected wrong messages in its value system that show men exhibiting tendencies to sexism, such as control, strength, and power, as acceptable behavior and warranting great respect. Both women and men are conscripted to believe that a man represents power and authority and he has the most ability to lead and be in control of affairs in domestic or global spaces.

Women want to be recognized, equally represented, and desire to enjoy their rights to the fullest. However, in the midst of competing demands on society, not just from women but also from a diverse group of people advocating for their rights, this poses additional challenges and hurdles for women's agenda and their issues to be prioritized and appropriately addressed.

Society is so entangled with male chauvinism and misogyny

that it turns a blind eye to the fact that women constitute 50% of the world population, and no doubt are equal custodians of the world with God-given responsibilities and capabilities to manage and execute societal livelihood for human existence.

Throughout history women have stepped forward to embrace their femininity as human beings, asking no less treatment than that of a man. Doing so would create a better society where both genders can co-exist equally with their counterpart free of prejudice and bigotry.

One might say, "fair enough", but nothing happens to bring about the "Why" were women excluded from designing society? Centuries ago Margaret Brent stepped up to the plate demanding two votes, one being a landowner and the other as a legal representative during the year of 1647. She was refused, starting the battle which raged war on inequality and disparity of sexes such that on August 18th, 1920 in Tennessee, the 36th State of America kicked off the 19th Amendment - giving the right to vote not being denied on account of sex.

Questioning whether women and men have the same rights is no longer an issue, what can society do to pull down the barriers in order for a "woman" to discover her full potential as a human being of a natural order. We must frown on a society where the exclusion of women, and the tradition showing men are superior and women inferior remains. This is the ideal for which women are still fighting, with no collateral damage except self-preservation.

Above all, for good to prevail over evil, equality over inequality, and right over wrong, men and women must stand side by side speaking up loud enough. How loud? Loud enough to have the bells of liberty and freedom sound in our homes and in every nook and cranny of society.

Under the Equal Rights Law of the USA, the Civil Rights, 42 U.S. Code, Chapter 21, Subchapter 1981, it states:

"All persons within the jurisdiction of the United States shall have the same right in every State and Territory to make and enforce contracts, to sue, be parties, give evidence, and to the full and equal benefit of all laws and proceedings for the security of persons and property as is enjoyed by white citizens, and shall be subject to like punishment, pains, penalties, taxes, licenses, and exactions of every kind, and to no other." Note, this clause is not talking about discrimination of color or ethnic background, but the equality of "All".

The many complications of understanding the law is taking a pathway where the intent of it gets lost in translation and increases frustration. It brings about personal emotional conflicts, especially when male dominance becomes stronger. As multiple genders speak up for their own equality and society is backsliding on removing negative behaviors toward "a woman", society is reaching its homophobic state. It will be an incorrect denial on the part of anyone to think that society itself, in its structural arrangements to give direction, guidance, and assurance for the growth and development of the human race, is not looking to sustain the image of the male as the most superior.

As a consequence, these lopsided walls of perception and belief are continually tearing down the fabric of gender equality and women's rights, thus raising men to think lesser of a woman. The increased violence against women, their marginalization, and other unhealthy diminishing behaviors inflicted on women says volumes about society.

The glass encased tomb of women's subordination and men's superiority ultimately will not be shattered if society remains engulfed in its state of patriarchal establishment. No woman should have to live a life of fear or as a shadow without visibility, voice, relevance and the freedom to be who she is.

Wow! Yes, a big wow and a bit fuzzy. But in all this, women are focused on celebrating their femininity. They are proud in their own skin as women, and do not want to become manly to enjoy the same rights as a man. They do not want to be validated by men or be recognized that they are worthy and productive human beings in order to feel good about themselves.

A society thrives even more when voices are not just heard but are also considered valuable and are incorporated in the grand scheme of national development and the betterment of society. It must be recognized that those voices are integral and equal, providing balance on the scale of humanity.

The feminist movement is about eliminating patriarchy, claiming the rights of women, and gender equality. It is a struggle against giving reasoning to what defines manliness and womanliness. After all, upscaling the voice of reasoning that "I am a woman", a human being in existence is cardinal to gender equality and women human rights.

Women's rights have its equal in human rights, as human rights are equality itself enshrined with civil liberties. All a woman wants is to take her rightful place among the ranks of humankind and make use of the opportunities, potentials, and talents free of prejudice and enslavement. The best in human beings is never fully realized if society restricts and puts them in a box in which they are limited and go no further than they are told.

This is another reason why, when asked "Whose shoe is it anyway?", it becomes a difficult answer to accumulate in its truest form, because we do not see, but feel, what has been brought or taught within our daily lives about women, just "not" an equal.

Equality has a foundation in creation that is inseparable to the human being lying in these words, that all are created equal to have dominion over the earth. Anything outside of that is man-made and not divine. Society may have selectively and pleasantly chosen to forget who a woman is, and in turn sees women through the lenses of a misogynistic compass with no accountability to the consequences thereof, Chromo-zoning a way of life that is morally wrong and detrimental to the well-being of women.

We now see how it happens and that women are put under the footsteps of men and systems which embody a way of destructive norms and chauvinistic values. But it is not enough to *persuade society that the female is under threat* in a way that gender inequality is on the platform of life and is a growing epidemic of evolution with minimal bearing and unclear direction.

Concrete actions must be taken because inequality doesn't readily give free direction or enjoyment of rights or choice to women. Even free to make choices, it is harder to put on a "man's role" and be successful, but it's easier for a man to take on a "woman's role" and be very successful. Why is that? This is where supremacy reigns, an indication that we have been orientated or socialized to think in this fashion.

In the teachings of certain religions, a woman is considered as a weaker vessel and incapable of doing things that a man does or can handle. What's more interesting is that the intellect of a woman is assumed to be less in comparison to her male counterpart. Although it is scientifically proven that women have a higher IQ than men, it is not in the interest of men, the custodians of patriarchy, to acknowledge and elevate this fact. Furthermore, had it not been the wisdom, inner strength, and resilience of women since ages of old, this world would be a more dangerous place.

Throughout centuries and in our lifetime, women have risen to greatness, and led with boldness, wisdom, and courage, overcoming the impossible, to leave legacies that men have yet to surpass. Witness: Joan of Arc, Queen Isabella, Queen Elizabeth I, Pocahontas, Queen Anne, Susan B. Anthony, Florence Nightingale, Harriet Tubman, Clara Barton, the founder of the Red Cross, Annie Oakley, Marie Curie, Gail Laughlin, Helen Keller, Eleanor Roosevelt, Margaret Mead, Mother Teresa, Rosa Parks, Margaret Thatcher, Anne Frank, Opera Winfrey, who now owns her own syndicated network, and the first woman to be elected President in an African country, Ellen Johnson Sirleaf of Liberia, and many more.

Yes, these women symbolized the truth that there is nothing a man can do that a woman cannot also do; moreover, that women are so strong that words can't break them. So, we must break the chains on women's progress and see that it is not expedient to ignore the power and intellect of a woman, or to continue to hold the gender glass above her head without its shattering. By neglecting to take concrete steps, beyond words of appeasement and solidarity, means men want our countries, communities and systems to remain as they are: pro-male and anti-female; that women rights are not human rights and gender equality is not crucial to the development of nations and advancement of the world.

This is a self-inflicted burden brought on by men of might, power, and small mindedness in regions of the world. People of conscience, irrespective of nationality, ethnicity, or religious background, should be the moral voice of society and together rebuild society on the foundation of human dignity, equality, and justice.

Is this doable? Possible? Breakable? you may ponder. But remember the saying 'where there is a will there is a way.' It takes only the power of agreement in the mind to do the impossible for herein lies your willpower.

I am inclined to bring another face to the table of women that have done the impossible for women's struggle. She is Funmilayo Ransome Kuti of Nigeria, a feminist and activist who is also a political leader who took part in the rooting of the Abeokuta Women's Union (AWU) movements and the Women's International Democratic Federation (WIDF).

The Abeokuta Women's Union led the Abeokuta Women's Revolt, a women's resistance movement in the late 1940's. This revolt was against the unfair and discriminatory taxation that was enforced by the Nigerian colonial government on women since January 1st, 1918. They had the privilege of working in the manufacturing industry which soon became an oppressive condition.

Funmilayo Ransome Kuti led about a thousand women in a protest march. This was all after a number of women stopped paying their taxes and were soon fined or jailed.

Shortly, this protest, like many others that we see today,

ended up in brutal and harsh treatments, including tear gas and beatings which made their situation worse when they couldn't cooperate to settle the matter. There went on a struggle until November 30th, 1947, when over ten thousand women demonstrated outside Alake's palace, singing harsh but meaningful songs such as *"a man uses his penis as a mark of authority, and now women will use their vagina as a source of revenge"*.

This went on for almost 24 hours, November 29th, 1947 to the following morning of November 30th, 1947 when an understanding was reached, with promises made to the women and, most importantly, and momentum was given to their stance for equal treatment within their rights.

True to the nature of patriarchy, the men would not succumb to doing right by the women, despite reaching a compromise and making promises. Neither would they allow justice to prevail. Having the power and authority, they refused to budge on abolishing direct taxation aimed toward the women.

Nonetheless, the women didn't give up and by January 3rd, 1949, two years after the Abeokuta Women's Union had celebrated a victorious legacy, that we have seen today a King giving up his throne in the palace and the system of the Sole Native Authority changed. The new system provided four women with positions inside the administration of the SNA in Nigeria.

Here again, history reminds us of the ugly head of patriarchy, the form and shame in which it comes to devour women and disrupt lives. The moral of this is that women overcame fear and showed that there is power in unity of purpose and no glass is too thick to shatter if we agree. It all starts in the mind.

Women in general are not trying to take over or wear and walk in a man's shoes as it is perceived when women demand gender equality. To the contrary, women love to be in their own shoes and to feel equally comfortable walking in them and going wherever their legs can reach. No matter what country a person resides in, if positive attributes continue to be associated with only men, society will remain bleak to the causes of women.

A woman should not have to go through extreme measures to prove that she is worthy and endowed with natural gifts and talents as a human. She is not looking to dominate, conquer, or rule another human being. She is looking for the equality that replaces the dominant role or control factor. When both the man and woman are parallel to each other, there is no sense of "I must be in control".

We are faced with many barriers to getting society to be fair and balanced, and to eradicate enabling factors that perpetuate the abuse of women, their rights, and gender equality. It feels like a steel wall, purposely designed and built to keep women out, meanwhile giving the impression that the wall is penetrable.

This is no coincidence nor is it a random thought. This is how chauvinism works. Yet, ironically this is how the society has been working and been establishing its dominant mark for a very long time.

Chauvinism has gone beyond gender equality and human

rights where pride rules as an arrogant and egotistical tyrant bent on proving an acceptance of bigotry and narrow-mindedness when it comes to women; that women are no more than service to men.

Our societies are built on the sweat, tears, and blood of those seen and doomed as lesser human beings; the poor, the vulnerable, and the weak. Obviously, these are attributes conferred on a woman which provides motive for a man's claim to superiority over her. Oh, is it unjust? Is it really that bad? Are women not just exaggerating or a bit dramatic? Well, know this, when a woman wakes up to the comprehension that she can become something more, something beautiful, victorious, special, powerful, and unbreakable, then she is labelled by society whose intent is to subdue her with fear, for she will not yield to submissiveness.

It is so hard to draw back the line of dominance and proceed, with innocence, to show that humanity is equality, that men are human, and women are human beings too. Her tender appearance is not weakness, and this doesn't mean that a tender appearance is uniquely feminine.

It is wrong for society to portray women as only nurturers and caregivers, and not as builders and architects of our world. When we create a society thinking as a whole, within one community, as the human race, we act collectively and are measured as a unit of one, a thought of one, as sharer of one; an equal as of one.

If we separate ourselves in humanity as a single, then we're alienating ourselves from the equation of humanity as one who either thinks for oneself or is the weak link that has been separated from the whole. The point is, the only real reason for the separation from one another is want of dominance or supremacy, that one will be more superior or authoritative over others. We are left with a society bent on segregation, becoming a barrier, losing its grip and being passive about male supremacy.

The voice of reasoning gets contorted, twisted and knotted up in viewpoints, lost in the shuffle of our thought patterns. When we encounter things in our daily lives, how do we react? Encountering is normal but our reaction to situations could be based on how we were brought up to see things and what we are conditioned to accept as right or wrong.

From birth we have been taught to interact, think, and behave in certain ways yet not conditioned to know that women have rights. Among those are the rights of choice and self-determination, actualization to become whoever she wants to be. No matter the circumstances and difference of opinions, the question should always be 'whose life is it anyway?' It is the woman's! And therefore, society must change for a woman to become who she is meant to be in comfort, rights, and equality.

Whose shoe is it anyway!!! Rights and Choice

CHAPTER 4

Let Me Breathe
Kill Suppression, Oppression, Sexism

If a person does know the difference and still makes a sound decision on what is wrong, and not on what is best and just, then male or female it doesn't matter. Bigotry becomes its blossom of prejudice, an influence that is not supposed to be tolerable. And now this is why we wonder about where women go from here. H*ere* they are trapped in a social network of those who believe that women are less than men which escalates into verbal, physical, and emotional abuse toward women.

This is what women around the world are waking up to! It does not matter if we like it or not. This is the real world that we see and feel every day, knowing that a perverse lineage or ancestry has gone astray in society, attacking and choking the life out of a woman and making this beautiful precious flower wither.

Rap Artist, Lupe Fiasco, stated it right, back in 2012, with the lyric titled, "Bitch Bad," that the words continually being fed, even into children, are condoning disrespect, showing who is in control under the family roof. We can't stop what they see and hear, but we can teach right from wrong and strengthen ourselves as positive role models for younger women to know that they are human too.

In this way, a young girl and a woman may have that dignity that has been so stripped away from them by our society. The society rising to vulgar, emotional, and physical abuse, and stamping a defeated label on the woman is neither laughable nor entertaining to watch.

This type of transformation does play another negative and significant role that makes society a gatekeeper to the suppression, oppression, and abuse of women.

Somehow, we are led to wonder about this woman as a human being. Yet we are baffled but not really shocked that there is so much against her. It is almost inexplicable and much less desirable. That is why Women's Rights are and should remain valuable. It cannot be displayed through the appearance of ignorance, nor should it be displayed as a joke or just a long-winded fad since its opening introduction in 1848. There was a lot at stake involved for the women of this era in openly standing up and having a voice.

In 1972, an album was released by an Australian-American artist by the name of Helen Reddy. A song titled, "I Am Woman, *Hear Me Roar*" became an empowering national and international liberation anthem for the women's liberation movement. A song which resonated with all women of color, ethnic background, and religion who are not going to pretend that nothing is going on, that everything is alright. There is a movement in which all women must stand up and be accounted for as human beings. Her song of inspiration and empowerment lets a woman know that she is strong, that she's invincible, and that she is woman. This song also was in the closing credits for the Movie, titled "Stand Up and Be Counted", about the liberation of women.

The songwriter's actual intent for this song was for others to know that whatever she was going through, she was still standing strong, and everyone else can too. During the counterculture era, they took flight and sprouted wings, soaring directly into the prevailing arms of women, those who needed to stand up for themselves, individually and collectively.

This single-mindedness was the hope of a union with the population of women acting as one voice, to be heard from the kitchen and onto the floors in the political arena where their voices can be much more than opinionated, valued as law in the eyes of Civil Rights and Human Rights.

Couldn't this be something that we missed but can be

remembered as something so precious and worth fighting for?

The Convention on the Elimination of All Forms of Discrimination against Women (CEDAW) states that equal rights for women are basic principles of the United Nations. Its preamble is the confirmation of the goals pertaining to "faith in fundamental human rights in the dignity and worth of the human person, in the equality of men and women". The Optional Protocol on Human and People's rights on the rights of Women in Africa mandates equal rights for women and States actions for affirmation to ensure equal representation of women in governance and eradicate harmful cultural practices including Female Genital Mutilation.

This does lead us to the Universal Declaration of Human Rights that everyone is entitled to equality, the right to fundamental freedom, and the enjoyment of human rights without any distinction.

The Commission on the Status of Women (CSW) was formed within this International Bill of Human Rights to proclaim its awareness on how all manner of women ought to be treated fairly, without partiality, or the appearance of it bringing back the *Women's Rights Movement* where there was a *Declaration of Sentiments* that showed how women were being treated.

There were eighteen grievances that the America revolutionary forefathers had listed within their Declaration of Independence from England. But, Elizabeth Cady Stanton had her own drafted version which states that "The history of mankind is a history of repeated injuries and usurpations on the part of man toward woman, having in direct object the establishment of an absolute tyranny over her. To prove this, let facts be submitted to a candid world."

Some of the specifics read:

- Women were not allowed to vote
- Women had to submit to laws when they had no voice in their formation
- Most occupations were closed to women and when

women did work they were paid only a fraction of what men earned

- Women were not allowed to enter professions such as medicine or law
- Women had no means to gain an education since no college or university would accept women students
- With only a few exceptions, women were not allowed to participate in the affairs of the church
- Women were robbed of their self-confidence and self-respect, and were made totally dependent on men

It didn't take much for Mrs. Elizabeth Stanton a housewife and mother to initiate and launch a women's revolution. All it took was her and a few women, friends of hers, congregating in their own little in-house tea party get-together, socializing and . . . *Voila!* A revolt begins to take root and grab onto a foundation it can build on. She had her own discontentment issues that she wanted to address concerning her own limitations during the time of America's new democracy. That's all it takes, just a handful of people with grievances and someone to lead the way, or at least someone to open the door and set the tone for change.

But it didn't stop there because it marked the beginning of the Women's Rights Movement on July 13th, 1848, in upstate New York. Inspiring huh?! Yes, she didn't stop there, but continued the draft which also read:

"Now, in view of this entire disenfranchisement of one-half the people in this country, their social and religious degradation, in view of the unjust laws above mentioned, and because women do feel themselves aggrieved, oppressed, and fraudulently deprived of their most sacred rights, we insist that they have immediate admission to all the rights and privileges which belong to them as citizens of the United States."

What was interesting was, years after the Revolutionary War, unfair treatment of women was considered normal which had a negative effect on both European-American women and enslaved Black women during those times.

Of course, those who wore the invisible words of bigotry and supremacy across their chest wouldn't let this now published draft go unnoticed. It was mocked, ridiculed, and laced with shame against the media who published it. And get this, the women's rights movement was only one day old; but that didn't stop most women from coming forward and staking their claim.

Still, women are constantly striving to break that glass of oppression and tyranny. It keeps on getting thicker and thicker with suppressive and oppressive tendencies, even in our social language, and in the way we speak to women, showing signs of disrespect.

This needs to end with a permanent solution so that all women across the nations, young and old, can hear each other's roar and come up with more solutions to the madness. Even the humiliation of knowing that in many, if not all, religious institutions where equality supposedly stands on the Word of God, the scale of rights and equality is unbalanced.

Leveling the playing field is to harmonize the gender equation and move away from elements that disenfranchise and choke women to death. We are watching more and more the increase in violence against women, the decisions weighing on abortion choices, the early girlchild marriage, the sexual and domestic abuse is slowly being suppressed and counted as a mere nuisance to society.

This is how the legacy of women's rights has been orchestrated to be thrown into the toilet. Women are cornered to fade away in the shadows, afraid to breathe for fear of physical and verbal cruelty. This simply cannot be! We are awake enough now to know that for decades women have been in a constant battle for rights and entitlements that include personal security and living without fear of your voice having been strangled and your life deemed expendable.

Where will the light shine? It is where we are awake enough

to see how society has turn our minds into believing that for women, subordination and oppression is a way of life, that the standards set by society in regard to morality, social consciousness, and law of nature can be discounted when it is applicable to women.

We have to rethink our perception and come to the understanding that we must excel in womanhood and disallow privilege, deviant and tyrannical behaviors. It is wrong for society to become accustomed to this type of social order and to claim it as true liberty and freedom.

Let Me Breathe!!! Kill Suppression, Oppression, Sexism

CHAPTER 5

In Equality We Rise
Women's Rights is Centerline

Having equal rights for women is not the same as wanting to have equal rights for women. There are many different types of illusions that would indicate society is okay with the way things are while women sense a roaring across society because something has considerably failed - that a female is no more than a minority voice that quietly whispers in the night.

This is a thought among men who have experienced the liberty of freedom, the rights of freedom, and know the enjoyment within freedom itself. If you're living the dream of gender equality that's great! But, if you are feeling a little different about things or are conscious of what you're going through or seeing what women are going through, then perhaps there wasn't that much enjoyment of gender equality after all.

It is not really equal that some part of humanity has been stripped away from society.

Gender equality is about seeing men and women as equal human beings with equal rights. Women's rights are the centerline for the fulfillment of rights enshrined.

Laws are created to govern and preserve individual rights and serve as a moral compass to know the right from the wrong upon which they abide. Inside those laws we find rights like the right to vote, freedom of speech, equality and reproduction.

But we have come to know that all the talk about gender equality by governments and society as a whole does not stop women's rights being torn down. Women's rights came about to outline the basis for women's equality in every aspect of life.

It became a movement and a centerline in order for women to be able to speak for themselves. This movement has been portrayed as a new, foreign or western ideology but, in essence, it is a very old and returning voice. Long before women were granted the right to vote, it preordained the changes in laws that we are seeing today. This centerline is women's rights.

Women are expected to be satisfied and take pride in the progress and achievements they have made over the decades as compared to centuries ago. Furthermore, women should be happy that they have gained the recognition of being equal to men, that their dreams and aspirations and the fight for equal rights are pushed above the horizon and are now at the doorway of achievement.

This tells of a society that has taken women for granted throughout history, whether it's in the law, in a development plan, or in policies causing lost opportunities from women.

What we should be looking at from this point is what

changed in our society that the natural order of humanity split, thus giving us a caution to think about what's really going on in the world or did women's roar just go silent for a moment.

There are a number of laws throughout past and present times that have been formulated, changed, and mistranslated to discourage women in finding and redefining themselves. To represent oneself as a human, deserving dignity and more, not an object to be used and discarded.

In religion, during the 15th and 16th centuries, the Medieval Canon Law, which is composed of ordinances and regulations which were made by ecclesiastical authority, encouraged men to collectively punish their wives in public instead of killing them if they became disobedient or were caught in adultery.

The law supports male domination reigning in legal authorities and power of society, so women have to understand that this is a collective force agreeing on the same male agenda, the patriarch.

A patriarch is a man having power over a woman with the authority to control, break the will, spirit of the mind, and body to achieve submission. Now, here comes women's rights - the centerline to help diminish male dominance, abusive laws, and harmful cultural practices that are an injury to women. Women can only rise to their fullness when society dismantles gender inequalities and features the position of women as second to none.

What we are discovering is a provocative yet profound truth and questionable answer which expands our knowledge of gender equality. Within our personal curiosity, we share conclusive and convincing arguments that, since nations declared independence and expressed a cardinal rule that all peopled are created equal, women on the most part are not in that equation.

We have to understand that there are more steps to take, and more mountains to climb if we are to show the world that we, as women, are also human. The centerline of women's rights is the ability and the power to bring about a change in laws that negatively affect or disable the human rights of women. Laws were created to govern and preserve the rights of freedom. It is the legal principles of those laws that our moral compass dictates the right from wrong upon which it abides.

If women do not speak for themselves, nothing will really change. The only change that will be made is the increase of male dominance around your world as a woman. The centerline - women's rights must remain strong and maintained as one voice.

In Equality We Rise!!! Women's Rights is Centerline

CHAPTER 6

At the Feet of Every Woman
Find Yourself

For decades women have come together to fight side by side, holding under the banner of women rights specific causes: gender equality, human rights, peace and Justice around the world. This could not have come about if women were not discriminated against and made to feel that they were second class citizens with restricted rights and freedoms in society, having no place equal to a man.

It is in these circumstances and shared experiences that women activists and feminists have come to identified with, and they build a bond of camaraderie and solidarity around their common interest. They carry a torch a reflection for all other women to follow with the hope that the flame is not dampened.

In personal and general struggles for self-realization, women have found inspiration and courage from women before them who overcame hurdles to become champions for women causes. Those today who have struggled to climb surmountable mountains to carry on the fight, rise to power and become successful women.

We would be amiss, however, to think that the gains and successes women are making are opening more doors. To the contrary, doors keep closing tighter and tighter as men fear losing control, a fear that has the propensity to take us backwards and make it harder for women to actualize their aspirations and ambitions. Believing the illusion that she is not destined for power and authority, that she is only the face of a male shadow, male dominance still rules

In the Huffington Post, when Marsha Blackburn was rumored to be in consideration as a running mate for Donald Trump in order to bring in the women's vote she was interviewed by BBC's Katy Kay. After viewing Megan Kelly's question to Trump on what she would say about the language Trump used, "You call women you don't like fat pigs, dogs, slobs and disgusting animals," the Congresswoman from Tennessee replied, "You say, 'I wish you had not done that.' Whether it was working in a male dominated profession or serving here in Washington, you have people who say inappropriate things. I think most women are like me. You've heard enough of it through the years that you don't excuse it, and you don't embrace it, but you push it aside."

It shows a double-blinded position that women are placed in, and it has an effect on one's sense of self. But you need the job, you need the money, and until a better opportunity comes along, you endure.

This is a vulnerability that lies at the feet of every woman.

No room to breathe, no workplace to set down their purse and perform a job without looking over her shoulder or surrendering. Also called conceding, it brings about a forceful choice to survive in a world of dominating power. This is the illusion women must learn without fear to overcome!

The illusion that women are not destined for greatness and are weak has grown into threats and all types of sexual misconduct. But, if you think women are the weaker sex, you better wake up and smell the coffee. Women are tougher than men and have a longer life, in spite of all that they have endured.

Don't be fooled though. Living in our society today, with the world turning its head in different competing directions, the pressure is on to ensure women's survival. This means women do not have the luxury of allowing their lives to be controlled by their circumstances.

It is your God-given right as a human being to be treated humanely, with dignity and equality. Both men and women need to accept change, a change that sees both a woman being rightly equal and having a better world, intertwined and inseparable. This also requires women being prepared to broaden all of our views, shifting our mindset to become better and embrace a truthful answer within ourselves in order to become more than just a voice of change, but a voice for positive actions.

Because at the feet of every woman lies our common experiences and interest which forged a bond, so must each person discover herself to be empowered to take back her power. She must break away from the social constructs that are hindrances and that limit her ability to grow.

As we see each other passing by every day, we must not forget that we still have a long hill to climb to be treated as equal to men. Women are 80 percent the minority in politics. In business circles, women represent only 14.2 percent of CEOs. Women continue to receive an unbalanced and lower pay grade than men in the same position. Twenty out of twenty-four women are also more likely to be subjected to domestic violence between the ages of 18-44, including some becoming sexually assaulted. Poverty has taken its toll also, seeing more single women with children where six out of ten survive at or below the poverty level.

This is a major challenge to the empowerment of women and an impediment to their development which should raise the moral consciousness of each person to change this paradigm, for there is more that binds us than divides us.

Again, it is important to find out who we are as individuals and then represent each other as a collective whole.

At the Feet of Every Woman!!! Find Yourself

CHAPTER 7

A World Visa
Violence, Sex, Abuse

The number of men accused for acts of sexual offenses, including sexual harassment, has risen over the years, particularly amongst the rich and powerful, with little dispute to these allegations. The argument by powerful men is that it is just a few sick men. Furthermore, this acknowledgement of its prevalence and the efforts being made to stop these violent acts from occurring through legal action or public naming and shaming of these men that are accused, is regarded as a plus for women.

In a political arena that is unfriendly to women in a society in which men are the dominant figures, entrusted with more power including control and assess to wealth, women are often subdued, and their dignity stripped away.

This is not a one country itemized incident. It is a worldwide global escalation of women's oppression by a sustained patriarchal society needing to keep women away from natural existence, weakening their rights and undermining the continual fight to reject sexism.

We have a society that is orchestrated to give power to men and allow them to rise onto private and national platforms of leadership through which they enjoy the trust and covenants of their people, nations, communities, and families. However, instead of living up to the expectations befitting leadership positions and ranks, many men are found to be engaged in despicable acts of violence, sexual exploitations, and various forms of abuse. As long as society continues to associate power of authority with men, giving them opportunities to leverage on that power and authority, it increases and sustains their economic strength, social status, and perpetuates the culture of inequality that represents women as inferior, as sex symbols for the pleasures of men. Sexual violence and other offenses against women will continue to escalate with impunity.

Genuine efforts and commitment to change the imbalances of power between men and women, including effective punitive measures, must be made to deter sexual abusers and acts of violence. Any form of violence and sexual abuse, publicly or privately, demands our collective voices to condemn and bring perpetrators to justice.

We must press on and persevere even when confronted with a predominantly male justice system and a legislative body of government who often have trouble overcoming their own biases to take appropriate actions to address cases of sexual offenses and violence against women.

Women security and bodily integrity is a development

agenda and not a man's self-gratifying agenda that has the propensity to downgrade the mainstream of society and ruin the lives of women. The weight of these ruins is far more costly to repair than prevent.

There is a familiar saying that "prevention is better than a cure." So true! That is why no one should stand aside or turn a blind eye to a crippling and enabling society with poisonous venom which subjects women to the whims and sexual caprices of men. The setting up of different standards for men and women, the representation of women in both private and public spaces as inferior, and the silent acceptance of wrong behavior and attitudes towards them have the propensity to mimic one another amongst younger males in present and future generations to come.

When a cordial interaction between a male and a female turns into sexual aggression, even after she says the word "No!" or "Please, I do not wish to be bothered," it often leaves the woman speechless and emotionally shocked.

This is a classic example of an uninvited sexual encounter where the man interprets that as sexual consent and ceases to prey on her. Exhibiting might of power with a motive to subdue and intimidate, not caring if they said no, were married or single, but just exhibiting the self-sexual gratification. It is an abuse of power and he knows that he can get away with it.

The 2017 RAINN (Rape, Abuse & Incest National Network) statistics show that there are almost 300,000 progressions of all nationalities and genders that have been victims of sexual assault.

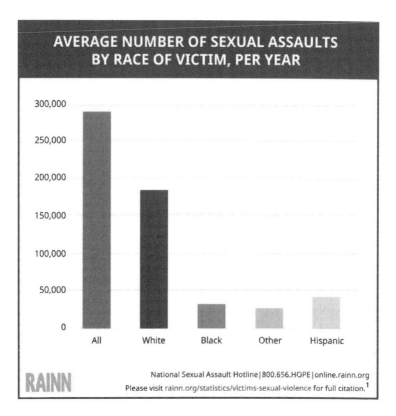

According to the United Nations (UN Women), it is said that "35 percent of women worldwide have experienced either physical or sexual violence by a partner or non-partner at some point in their lives while some national studies also show that up to 70 percent of women have experienced physical and sexual violence from an intimate partner in their lifetime."

Women continue to be in the cusp of violence and sexual abuse from century to century like an ongoing, non-stop religion of its own cult of male dominance. What this tells us is, it does not matter the level of education or social status a woman has, whether rich, poor, old or young, most have been violated.

There is no category of men exempted from committing this sexual and bodily harm on women, even in the highest levels of the political arena where kings, presidents, and high-ranking leaders are supposed to be leading with a moral example.

This is not the kind of world for male generations to model under or for future female generations to succumb to. We cannot veil tolerance and continue to reenact historical scenes of abusive and domineering power toward and against women.

A World Visa!!! Violence, Sex, Abuse

CHAPTER 8

Breaking the Code of Silence
It's His Shame Not Yours

Men have claimed a position of superiority and played the role since the beginning of time, despite the fact that it has never been proven scientifically or religiously. Society disregards that both female and male were created as equal human beings in the sight of God to have dominion and rule over the earth.

A *disregard* of this fact is the basis on which men feel privileged and claim the right to treat women in a demeaning and reckless manner. This establishes a negative behavioral pattern as an acceptable norm embedded in society.

The biblical saying that the woman is the weaker vessel is interpreted as her being fragile, helpless, having lesser capabilities, not endowed with abilities equal to a man, and therefore a reason to make her live at the mercy of the man.

Governments and world bodies make pronouncements, laws, and resolutions in favor of women being equal citizens and having all rights. We celebrate these declarations. But the failure to turn words into concrete actions that could transform the mindset of how men perceive women, from the highest office all the way down to the dinner table, gives rise to misogynistic behaviors.

With this comes a false sense of control and authority which allows a man to rear the beast within himself and exercise power over her. Any type of power over someone against their will is considered holding them hostage.

This is where society has a deaf ear to the plight of women held hostage and in bondage by misogyny founded on the backs of formal, informal, traditional, and religious education. Whether intentionally or not, the importance of power for man in relation to a woman is taught as fundamental to "manliness".

Now with this kind of socialization, be it in a public, social, religious, domestic relationship or interaction, men are sure to exhibit a reckless and growing pattern of control and anger, often leading to verbal, emotional, sexual, and physical violence, especially when he doesn't get what he wants.

This is well known as the term *"Abuse" and it* destroys the mental and physical life of a woman and places her in a haphazard, jeopardizing position. The men with such ingrained tendencies and narcissistic egos are obsessed with keeping a woman where he feels she belongs or teaching her "a lesson".

When a woman encounters a person like this in an intimate, causal, marital or non-marital relationship and is beaten, raped, sexually harassed and assaulted, she is ashamed, distrustful of herself and so scared that it overwhelms her into *Silence*.

It is in that silence that she becomes a victim, stripped of dignity, the joy of independence and the right to speak. She becomes a mere shell of a woman in a closet having to deal with the physical and mental torture of silence, fearing that it could happen again and again until she is dead.

The abuser gets his satisfaction, not only from committing the act, but in proving his manliness by subduing and lowering her, giving him more power over her body and mind to the point of threatening her very existence, if she tells.

Whether in platonic relationships, marriages, social interactions in private or public places, women having to speak out to say "No!" are getting throat-choked or knocked upside the head, or anything as vicious for that matter, to being someone's punching bag for a man's gratification.

We see how it unfolds in a work-related environment that places a woman in a very awkward position. It makes her feel like she can't just up and quit when she has children to support. An employer who pays her well enough but violates her, then forces her to be silent and accept the abuse because she does not want to be downgraded.

Women are victims of violence every day and everywhere. We hear about it on radios and television; read about it in newspapers; see it in entertainment, politics, home, work, religions, and communities.

Instead of society being for the whole of humankind, shows that it prefers that both men and women remain in respective positions where one is the devourer and other the devoured. This means a man can do anything he pleases to a woman and get away with it. This is not love for humanity. It is a reflection of society's distortion of creation, compassion, and tolerance and allows for evil and male pervasiveness.

In an attempt to break women and to make them see themselves as the scum of earth, this has rather strengthened their resolve more than ever to regain their power and refuse to be broken. Women are shaming rather than being ashamed. They are defeating emotional, psychological, and physical abuse by raising their voices and demanding accountability from society. No woman should have to wear a price tag on her future, for it will be trampled and blown over. Our future is not for the moment.

We cannot undo the past, but we can reclaim our power in the fullness of who we are as human beings, and change the negative waves roaring in our present to move forward into the future. The aggressor, the abuser, and the society that is brewing the worst nature of men must be stripped away.

Treating women in violent, abusive, and appalling ways is not a common thing. Neither should it be seen as normal at any place and time. Men should be removed from their self-arrogance in defiling a woman because he thinks he has the right to have control and *power* over a woman.

Society believes that there are more good men than bad, and because of that, tends to ignore the *cause and effect* of it, inflicting much pain and causing more problems than finding a solution. When society is in denial, the perpetrator feels justified and the woman is cornered into a code of silence. The cycle of violence never ends. Even those in trusted positions of leadership and power flex their muscles to take advantage of their positions, to continue and engage in sexual misconduct while covering tracks that would bring it forth.

Can you see how unjust and unfair our society is to women? It almost becomes unbearable to comprehend, let alone to face the fact that women have a very hard and long road to truly claim their humanity, being side-by-side equal to a man and live a violent free life.

Placing ourselves in a Woman Shoe perhaps demonstrates that it is all not as glamorous as some may be led to believe when women have "made it" in this world. On the contrary, most women have been in volatile and abusive positions since the beginning of time.

This, too, leaves the glass unshattered. Women are valuable, not vulnerable anymore, and not expendable. In this we must find our voices and rise up so high to say, "The wounding of my body and mind is not **my** blame. Shame, it is **his**." The punishment is on him to pay the price and live in misery.

Breaking the Code of Silence!!! It's His Shame Not Yours

CHAPTER 9

Politics, Power & Women
The Male Factor

Participating in politics is viewed as territory for men only. They are better prepared to understand the intricacies and controversies of its practice, which they feel entitles them to exclusive authority and power in political governance and other decision-making spheres.

Politics in Webster's definition is: the science and art of government, political affairs, methods, tactics, opinions to name a few, and factional scheming for power. It is no wonder politics as defined is the face of a man and functions as a club for men of vision, valor, and bravery, endowed with "Godly" wisdom, for engaging in governance and the conduct of affairs of society.

If politics is what it is, and society interprets its literal meaning to be that of a dirty, risky, scheming, tough and expensive game deserving of male participation but not women, it provides a platform to discourage, reject, and exclude them from getting involved and playing viable roles in political parties and governance.

The *school of thought* is that women are first and foremost born to be wives and mothers, to nurture their children and be a support to the man before anything else.

How then, the question is asked, can women dare to enter into such an exclusive domain and challenge the order of the "Creator"? How can they reject their place and fate in society which is to be governed instead of governing? How can they not be content having decisions made for them, rather than being decision makers?

Why can't she be happy being submissive rather than being rebellious, refusing to remain silent as a good woman is destined to be powerless, weak, subservient, to be conquered, led and ruled?

As you ponder on this, I hope you generate an open mindedness to see the necessity for changing the political and governing landscape, for ensuring women have equal participation and meaningful representation in government, and at various decision-making bodies in society as a whole. It is often said in socio-political debates and discussions that the personal is political, a phrase I have on many occasions used to encourage and inspire women to see politics and governance as relevant to their overall well-being.

It suits men to have control over women, and the most effective way of doing this is by having the power and authority over them, the power to decide and preside over our lives and the authority to enforce his commands.

Seeing this through your own personal lenses, meaning, looking at politics and governance from how it affects and impacts your life, will help bring a different perspective to your thinking.

Overcoming the misconception that politics is not for women and the fear of being labeled a politician, which carries a negative connotation, can only happen if you realize that it is a calculated attempt to keep women away from leadership positions and decision making.

Society has so many spider webs to entrap women in order to make sure they remain just where they want and need them to be. Women cannot be observers anymore and are not destined to be by-standers in political affairs of their countries or the world at large.

It is not enough to exercise only your right to vote, even though it is the most powerful tool in a thriving democracy. We must go beyond voting and use our votes to equalize women's representation in governance, ensuring the removal of unjust structures and frameworks, as well as unwholesome practices in the political arena.

The political is also personal. By this I mean, when a person gains authority, be it by election, executive appointment, or confirmation, they are invested with the power to have oversight on plans, policies, and enforcement. In so doing, they are not free of personal influences, upbringing, and social orientation in the dispensation of duties. It is therefore imperative to have women seated at the helm of political power, to guarantee not only their own agenda but also women's perspectives in the development and the well-being of other vulnerable people and society as a whole.

We have achieved a tiny crack in the glass ceiling of politics. Unfortunately, one step is taken forward then three steps go backwards, widening the gap that could decrease the gains made. It is almost like a thick glass hanging over women of all races, color, creed, ethnicity, religion, and origin who try to enter and excel within politics. Don't take it for granted that men are doing all they can to resist the sharing of power and authority.

In many African countries, the majority of political parties are established by men of means, and they dominate the hierarchy of those parties, with women given insignificant, non-decision-making posts. Like similar institutions around the world, women are marginalized and hardly included in the formulation of party, constitution, and other governing laws.

Most women enter into national politics and venture into public service with little knowledge about the workings and dynamics of governance. They are naive to the fact that men frown upon them, especially those already holding positions, those aspiring for political power, men in their own families, and not forgetting, religious and community leaders.

Very few women, if any, can say they have not experienced male chauvinism and abuses in their quest for political participation. Women are faced with this challenge every day, and because of this we should be encouraged to take our stand in a crucial role that would ensure women equal, unhindered engagement and participation in politics.

Now, an equal partnership does not necessarily require

dividing all responsibility and positions, 50-50, creating a platform and society where roles and capabilities are not defined by gender. Instead of upholding patriarchal tendencies and structures in politics, leadership, including assigning gender to behaviors, we must focus on removing stereotypical gender perceptions and expectations. Leadership and politics should not be synonymous with masculinity, just as taking care of the children, cooking, cleaning, should not be considered a woman's work and attribute.

Women need to become and continue to be a strong force in their nations and the world. A force for change so that misogyny and sexism will not be tolerated, and women will be treated as equal partners to make our societies better places to live in.

We can boast of brave women who have been homemakers or employed within civil, political, and military institutions that have managed to break through toward a political life and stood against male oppression. They are a beacon of light among women, including those who are not able to endure in present political times because politics still remains in the hands of men.

More than ever, we need women in leadership and political governance. We need to rise and strive to barrel down the various layers of patriarchal family and structures that have been nurtured which emphasize hierarchy, authority, and gender roles for men, women, girls and boys that limit us within our own democracy.

It is the 21st century and women must be seen as a gender with astute and unique political abilities that can no longer be put off like a candlelight, despite the misogynistic behavior and dominance of men in political spheres.

The more men refuse to wake up from the false illusion that politics is not for women, the more fragile and unsafe society will be as they become afraid of their humanity. When every female voice of silence begins responding loudly and audibly "No More!", then we can be somebody, then we can make a difference, and then we do not have to live in the shadows of fear any longer.

Yes, politics is for women too, and women can be very good

politicians and lead governments as well as society. Women in politics are a sign of the emergence of greater nations and a symbol of light. Like Tokyo's first female Governor, Yuriko Koike, who said with a smile, "My way of thinking is quite different from the previous governors. At least I'm not chauvinistic."

Ellen Johnson-Sirleaf, the first woman democratically elected President of Liberia, Africa's oldest independent Republic, for two six years term in office is the first of its kind on the continent of Africa. It *shattered the glass* of resistance and myth that only a man can become a President.

Then you have in Romania, Viorica Dancila, who was the first woman voted in as the Prime Minister; Trinidad, electing its first woman President, Paula-Mae Weekes; and Hillary Rodham-Clinton, who became the first woman to become a presidential nominee and candidate for the Democratic Party, one of two major political parties in the United States of America.

These women amongst many others are role models and

should give you an insight into the ability and foresight in facing challenges, striving to win, being able to hold steady political positions in government as well as other corporate or decision-making institutions.

This is not to say that the days of struggle for a woman to be treated as an equal are over. No. On the contrary, it is the opposite. But it is in fact slowly diminishing as we continue to rise up above oppressive political systems, fight political domination, remove negative elements of power and control such as exploitation, intimidation, emotional abuse, and shaming.

What these women have in common that we can adopt as a model path besides their femininity, is that they had to continue to struggle through many barriers and obstacles in order to continually crack that glass ceiling.

It is clear that to step in a woman's shoes is not enough. You have to walk in it to feel the pinch, tears, comfort, strength, courage and many other mind bogglers to accept that the ultimate good is a gender equal society where any human being can be who they wish to be, and enjoy their life without any nurtured hindrances, regardless if you are a man or woman.

There are many women today who are aspiring to positions in politics and who have set their mind to do so, irrespective of their current occupation, whether working at low level or high-profile jobs, running a small business like selling doughnuts or selling in a local market. There are those dealing with college bigotry, hatred, sexual harassment, domestic violence, and all kinds of dehumanizing vices who are showing the courage to shatter the glass ceiling in politics.

Women, like men, must live purposeful lives and look forward to being the best that they can be in life. They must be determined, against all odds, to accomplish their dreams and aspirations without falling under the guise of superiority and dominance that hold the progression of another human being captive for one's own self-purpose and gain.

Around the world in all cultural, ethnic, socio-economic, and political backgrounds, women are calling with a unified voice to remove the tyranny of patriarchy, loosen the chains of dominance, stop the violence against women, and build a society where women and men are equal partners in governance and decision-making spheres.

You've got to believe and be ready to stand firm as we all put ourselves in a woman's shoes and become human beings, first and foremost. Believe that we are equally formed with the same physical components of body parts, the exception being biological features that identify us as male and female, before seeing ourselves as men privileged to rule and conquer women, while women fight to free themselves from bondage and domination.

We must strive to move forward together. If you can step in the shoe and walk in **The Woman Shoe!** then together we can shatter the Glass Ceiling and be Winners!

Politics, Power & Women!!! The Male Factor

CHAPTER 10

Women Unite
Unity of Purpose

Unity is a revolutionizing form of not fighting among ourselves, believing it is through the intellect that we can become strong together and share the joy of success. If women are to move forward as a unit of one for their common good and goal, they must understand that unity matters and simply cannot be overlooked. For only then will women be able to cast down and destroy what society has taught and subconsciously mimicked throughout history.

It is unfortunate that women have to bear the burden of living in a patriarchal society.

It is not going to be pushed aside easily nor to fade away from existence with a stroke of the pen. It's more than just here to stay. It is in our faces every day with the evidence of some type of mistreatment towards women that creeps into plain view.

Even when those who try to ignore the situation of women for whatever reason and move on with their lives without wanting controversy, they cannot ignore the injustices, inequalities, and abuses women have suffered and continue to suffer as a result of patriarchal systems created to elevate men, to the detriment and disadvantage of women.

When you think about or read the list of rights for women, you would assume that our governments and governing institutions, men and society at large, take these rights seriously and are committed to enforcing them. Sadly, we have to learn that society needs a serious male adjustment to guarantee equal rights for women and gender equality.

This is a very bad discriminatory earmark that women can

band together on. We need one voice to fight against and uproot division, not leaving room for the powers that be and the enemies of women's progress to argue or rebuttal against. There can be no stronger case than this to warrant our solidarity and unity in one purpose.

Society is at a critical juncture where it is faced with competing forces and demands from diverse groups of people for changes to ensure their rights, for voices to be heard, and for concerns amongst others to not be swallowed up and excluded. Women cannot afford to be in disagreement about their own causes, which in my mind, so supersedes all others.

Women's rights are now becoming more difficult to establish as a whole because of certain obstructive perceptions and entrenched religious and cultural beliefs, despite laws stating that they are a key part of women's liberty, equality, and economic security. The political arena is becoming more vicious and expensive while politicians, mostly men, are less active in not hindering or deconstructing women's legal instruments or setting limitations on the mechanisms of implementation.

Women standing together in one accord are our power and this should not be a debate among us. This open paradigm of women's fight to be treated equal as human beings with equal rights has gone on long enough. It's time to regroup and strategize about how we can best serve each other in this journey back to the equality of our humanity, and fight towards taking our rightful place in society, enjoying our femininity, freedom, peace, and choice.

We need to look deeper inside to reject where society has positioned women as inferior to a man at all levels of functioning society, the control of our bodies and the socio-economic and political marginalization. We need to say, with definitive and conclusive answers, that men are not the superior being. Women have come a mighty long way in this struggle, and the more reason to realize that this fight cannot continue without our strength in unity.

We must never forget that our fight is not about each other. It is about claiming our right to be equal, to live victorious and fulfilled lives just as a man does.

We are stronger together than divided, and now is the time to strengthen our unity and fight harder for a level playing field, for women's well-being in society.

Women Unite!!! Unity of Purpose

Research ■ References

Credited to the Following Research References

(Note: The title references are correctly spelled in this fashion)

World News

iknowpolitics.org .... Ref. Article by CBS "Meet the women shifting the political landscape in Japan / Ref. Article by Newsweek "Africa's first elected woman president has transformed Liberia"

Time Politics

Time.com/newsletter/politics........Ref. Article by Ryan Teague Beckwith "Sexual Misconduct"

MsAfropolitan

www.msafropolitan.com ....Ref. Article on "African female icons that shaped history"

WomenSafe

www.womensafe.net... Ref. Domestic Violence

Wikipedia

en.wikipedia.org........   Ref. Women's Suffrage, Women's Rights, Title 42 USC, (AWU) Abeokuta Women's Revolt, Egba Alake, Butch and Femme, LGBT, I Am Women

The Washington Post

www.washingtonpost.com ....Ref. Article by Weiyi Cai "What Americans think about Feminism today" / Statistics & Surveys

RAINN

www.rainn.org .... Ref. Sexual Violence: Statistics, Sexual Harassment

Time Magazine

Time.com ...... Ref. Article by Nancy Gibbs "A Man's Right to Choose?"

Huff Post

www.huffingtonpost.com .... Ref. Article by Jennifer Rand "Equal Means Equal: Why Women Need The ERA" / Ref. Article by Fran Moreland Johns "Republican Men Against Women's Rights"

National Women's History Project

www.nwhp.org .... Ref. Women's Rights Movement

United Nations Human Rights

www.ohchr.org .... Ref. International Bill of Human Rights

OpenBible.info

www.openbible.info/topics .... Ref. Help Mate, The Role of Man

U.S. Equal Employment Opportunity Commission

www1.eeoc.gov//eeoc/publications .... Ref. Sexual Harassment

University of California, Santa Barbara Sociology

www.soc.ucsb.edu .... Ref. Sexual Assault

World News

www.nbcnews.com .... Africa's First Female President

Forbes

www.forbes.com/profile .... Ref. Ellen Johnson-Sirleaf

Encyclopedia Britannica

www.britannica.com .... Ref. Funmilayo Ransome-Kuti

Legal Information Institute (Cornell Law School)

www.law.cornell.edu .... Ref. Equal Rights Under the Law

HistoryNet

www.historynet.com .... Ref. Women's Suffrage Movement, Women's Rights, Famous Women

History

www.history.com .... Ref. Roman Emperor Caligula

PBS Detroit Public TV

www.pbs.org .... Ref. Women War & Peace

AfricaRenewal

www.un.org/africarenewal .... Liberia's Women Struggle

The Atlantic

www.theatlantic.com .... Ref. Rap's Long History of 'Conscious' Condescension to Women, Lyric of Lupe Fiasco

UN Women

www.un.org/womenwatch/daw/cedaw .... Ref. History of CEDAW Convention

Bible Hub

Biblehub.com .... Ref. Proverbs 21:2

The Guardian

www.theguardian.com .... Ref. Article by Martin Robbins "Why are women more opposed to abortion?"

National Women's Law Center

nwlc.org .... Ref. Abortion, Reproductive Rights, Civil Rights, Equal Pay

Made in the USA
Columbia, SC
17 October 2018